cloverleaf books™

Fall's Here!

Fall Pumpkins

Orange and Plump

Martha E. H. Rustad

illustrated by Amanda Enright

M MILLBROOK PRESS • MINNEAPOLIS

For my cousin Andrea—M.E.H.R.

Millbrook Press
A division of Lerner Publishing Group, Inc.
241 First Avenue North
Minneapolis, MN 55401 U.S.A.

Website address: www.lernerbooks.com

Main body text set in Slappy Inline 18/28.
Typeface provided by T26.

Library of Congress Cataloging-in-Publication Data

Rustad, Martha E. H. (Martha Elizabeth Hillman), 1975-
    Fall pumpkins : orange and plump / by Martha E. H.
Rustad ; illustrated by Amanda Enright.
      p.   cm. — (Cloverleaf books. Fall's here!)
    Includes index.
    ISBN 978–0–7613–5065–1 (lib. bdg. : alk. paper)
    1. Pumpkin—Juvenile literature. I. Enright, Amanda,
ill. II. Title.
    SB347.R87 2012
    635'.62—dc22
2010048310

Manufactured in the United States of America
1 – BP – 7/15/11

TABLE OF CONTENTS

Chapter One

Planting a Pumpkin Patch

It is spring, but I am thinking about **fall**. Let's **grow pumpkins** in the garden!

We make little hills in the soil. My hands get dirty! We plant two or three seeds in each hill.

Gardeners leave lots of space between hills in a pumpkin patch. Pumpkin vines can grow as long as 30 feet (9 meters).

We **dig moats** around the hills.
Then we water the seeds.
Sunshine warms the wet soil.

Later, the seeds crack open. Tiny roots grow down.

Moats around pumpkin hills help the soil stay wet. Wet soil is good for the seeds. It keeps them from drying out.

Two weeks pass. **Look!** I see tiny seedlings.

Little leaves grow from thin vines. The vines spread out.
Curly tendrils grab on to other plants or fences.

Pumpkins need long vines to grow. Small tendrils help the vines spread out. Sometimes gardeners guide the vines so they grow in the right direction.

Chapter Two

Flowers and Pumpkins

Now it is summer. **Look!**
I see **yellow flowers** on the vines.

Male flowers have pollen inside them.
Female flowers have a bump.

Buzz! Bees spread pollen
from one flower to another.
The bump will grow to be a pumpkin.

A pumpkin's female flower opens for only one day. The flower closes at the end of the day.

Little green pumpkins begin to grow. I water the plants every week. They start small and **grow bigger all summer.**

Leaves take in warm sunlight. **Sunlight becomes food** for the growing pumpkin plant.

Pumpkins take about one hundred days to grow. The biggest pumpkins can gain up to 25 pounds (11 kilograms) in a day.

Finally, it is fall. Harvesttime!

Cool air and short days tell the pumpkins to stop growing. Their skin turns orange. The leaves turn yellow. I'm ready to pick one!

Most ripe pumpkins are orange, but some kinds are green, white, blue, or red. All pumpkins are green when they first begin to grow.

15

Chapter Three

Using Pumpkins

Let's make **pumpkin pie**. **Splash!** We wash the pumpkin's skin.

Chop! We cut up the pumpkin and bake the pieces.

We scoop out the soft flesh and make a pie.

It smells delicious. **Yum!**

Buckskin, Small Sugar, and Winter Luxury are types of pumpkins that taste good in pies.

Let's carve a pumpkin. We cut open the top. We scoop out the seeds.

Pumpkins with a lot of ridges have a lot of seeds inside them. Smooth pumpkins have fewer seeds.

We cut out two eyes,
a nose, and a mouth.
Don't forget the candle.

Yikes! Our jack-o'-lantern looks spooky.

I save some of the pumpkin seeds. I will plant them next spring. I will think about my pumpkin patch all winter long.

How big will my **pumpkins** grow next year?

Atlantic Giant and Big Max pumpkins grow really big. The heaviest pumpkin ever weighed 1,725 pounds (782 kg). That's about as heavy as a cow.

Roasted Pumpkin Seeds Recipe

Ask an adult for help in the kitchen.

Ingredients:
1 ripe orange pumpkin
2 tablespoons oil or melted butter
1 teaspoon salt
½ teaspoon cinnamon
2 teaspoons sugar

Equipment:
sharp knife
large spoon
paper towels
measuring cups
2 mixing bowls
2 mixing spoons
2 baking pans
2 cooling racks
oven mitts
oven

1) Preheat oven to 300°F. Cut open the top of the pumpkin. Scoop out two cups of seeds with a large spoon.

2) Wash the stringy pumpkin flesh from the seeds. Lay the seeds out on paper towels. Let the seeds dry for 30 minutes.

3) Place the seeds in one mixing bowl. Add the oil or melted butter. Stir. Move half the seeds to the other mixing bowl.

4) Add salt to the first bowl. Stir well.

5) Add cinnamon and sugar to the second bowl. Stir well.

6) Spread the salty seeds on one baking pan. Spread the sweet seeds on the other pan.

7) Bake them for 15 minutes. Watch carefully! When the seeds are light brown, they are ready.

8) Take them out of the oven. Let the pans with the seeds cool on cooling racks. Taste both kinds. Which is your favorite?

GLOSSARY

delicious: good to eat

flesh: the part of a pumpkin you can eat

harvest: to gather crops that are ripe. Gardeners harvest ripe pumpkins in fall.

jack-o'-lantern: a pumpkin with a face carved into it and a candle inside

moat: a ditch around something, often filled with water

pollen: a tiny yellow dust made by flowers. Female flowers need pollen to make seeds.

ripe: ready to be picked and eaten

root: a part of a plant that grows underground. Roots pull up water from the soil.

seedling: a small, young plant

soil: dirt or earth. Plants grow in soil.

tendril: a narrow vine that curls around other plants, fences, or other objects and helps a vine grow

vine: a long stem that grows along the ground

Books

Dolbear, Emily J. *How Did That Get to My Table? Pumpkin Pie.* Ann Arbor, MI: Cherry Lake Publishing, 2010. This book features more information about how a pumpkin seed leads to a pumpkin pie.

Esbaum, Jill. *Seed, Seed, Sprout, Pumpkin, Pie*. Washington, DC: National Geographic, 2009. Take a look at this book's fall-season photos of pumpkin fields, jack-o'-lanterns, and more.

Nelson, Robin. *Pumpkins.* Minneapolis: Lerner Publications Company, 2009. This book explains the life cycle of a pumpkin with detailed color photos.

WEBSITES

Kids Gardening: Planting and Caring for Pumpkins
http://www.flowergardennews.com/Pumpkins-Growing_and_Caring_for_Pumpkins.html
Visit this site to learn more about growing your own pumpkins.

National Geographic Kids: Pumpkin Carving Tips
http://kids.nationalgeographic.com/Activities/MoreActivities/Pumpkin-carving
This site has step-by-step instructions for carving a pumpkin and a printable jack-o'-lantern pattern.

INDEX